MW01251806

.

© 2006 Albert Baker,PhD, Al Fischer, Clint Lewis and Ben Moore

Contents

About the Authors

Albert Baker, PhD.

Albert Baker is an internationally recognized expert in processes and techniques for mass customization with related advanced manufacturing technologies. His consulting clients have included General Electric, General Motors, Hitachi, the US Air Force, the US Army, and the Defense Advanced Research Projects Agency. He has lectured at numerous leading research institutions including the Massachusetts Institute of Technology (USA), Ecole Des Mines (France), and Ecole Polytechnique Fédérale de Lausanne (Switzerland).

Al Fischer

Al Fischer has led global engineering projects with Procter & Gamble for over 25 years. During this time, he led global product standardization efforts and global rapid prototyping efforts to institutionalize agile manufacturing. Al is also Founder and President of Accurate Product Development, LLC, a company providing Speed to Market for the non-woven industry and Founder and President of Configurable Manufacturing Systems.

Clint Lewis

For over 17 years Clint Lewis was instrumental in the start up and expansion of many product lines at Procter & Gamble such as Pampers, Rely, and Luvs. Experienced rapid progression through expanded "traditional" roles. Clint is the Founder and President of Lewis Group Consultants (LGC), an operations and technical manufacturing consultancy with a business philosophy over the past 17 years that centers on "Maximizing the Merger of People and Machinery."

Ben Moore

Ben Moore is the Founder and President of Agent Technologies, Inc. a firm specializing in eCommerce 4 Manufacturing (sm) through manufacturing consultants and software applications. His prior experience has included managing global software projects with Procter & Gamble and leading the Pampers.com e-Commerce initiatives.

Acknowledgements

I would like to thank my co-authors (Bert Baker, Al Fischer and Clint Lewis) who are three of the top manufacturing minds I have had the chance to work with over the years. Also, I want to thank Dave Stiles for helping me put this book together.

Thanks for all of your hard work.

Ben Moore

Introduction

This is a book for people who want to make a difference in their organizations – those who want to boldly innovate, dream and take risks, and not cower in fear because of changing circumstances.

For years writers have predicted the "death of American manufacturing". Over the years, we have seen this not only become a possibility, but a reality.

Most, unfortunately, have turned to hand wringing and whining as they discuss the future of American manufacturing. They lament the "good old days" when American industry provided for the world, or even of more recent times when the focus was on continuous improvement or lean manufacturing.

It would, of course, be an understatement to say that profound changes have happened within American manufacturing organizations in recent years.

Off-shoring has pitted traditional American manufacturing against cheap labor and low production costs. Rising expectations from sellers and consumers have brought added challenge and advances in technology have brought innovation as well as uncertainty.

In thinking about the current state of affairs, we are reminded of the phrase by Davis and Meyer, "Commerce used to be so simple". [1]

Another phrase that comes to mind is, "Toto, we're not in Kansas anymore."

The pace of change within surviving American factories has occurred at lightening speed. It is not just changes with competition and technology, it has occurred in nearly every part of the manufacturing process, from strategy life-cycles to "go-to market" cycles and product life-cycles.

We have written this book to help American manufacturers become more than survivors, but champions.

Although past change have challenged American manufacturing leaders; the future changes with vision will provide opportunities from which American leaders are uniquely situated to profit by.

This is a book for revolutionaries, those who "don't tinker at the margins; they blow up old business models and create new ones." [2]

We want to show you how to blow up old, antiquated models and use new models that work; that are inevitable and have first mover advantages.

We want to show you how to recreate your organization to achieve results through niche manufacturing and customized solutions to meet all of your customer's needs, increase productivity and decrease the time to launch.

This is a book for leaders.

Kouzes and Posner wrote that, "Leaders are pioneers. They are people who venture into unexplored territory. They guide us to new and often unfamiliar destinations." [3]
We believe that where American manufacturing is going will be difficult and unfamiliar, but leaders who are willing to pioneer the way will find the destination rewarding.

This is a book for visionaries.

Burt Nanus wrote that, "without leadership, an organization is like a lifeboat adrift in turbulent seas with no oars, no compass, no maps – and no hope." [4]

American manufacturing organizations need visionary leaders to help guide them through the uncharted waters of the future and to help them succeed where the words "failure" and "defeat" are too often the common refrain.

This is a book for fighters.

We are reminded of many years ago, when another leader faced some severe challenges. On June 4, 1940 in the midst of the German army's blitzkrieg through Europe, and only several days after the evacuation of his troops from Dunkirk, Winston Churchill rose in the British House of Commons and spoke this immortal words;

"We shall go on to the end. We shall fight in France, we shall fight on the seas and the oceans, we shall fight with growing confidence and growing strength in the air, we shall defend our Island, whatever the cost may be, we shall fight on the beaches, we shall fight on the landing grounds, we shall fight in the fields and in the streets, we shall fight in the hills; we shall never surrender." [5]

American manufacturing organizations have faced numerous challenges of late, but there is a bright future for those who chose to fight for their future.

Finally, this is also a book of hope.

Though recent trends in American manufacturing have not favored American manufacturers; the current trends that we describe especially favor American visionaries who embrace the trends to lead the current revolution.

Notes

[1] Davis and Meyer, *Blur*, (Reading, MA: Addison-Wesley) 1996. pg. 52.

[2] Gary Hamel, *Leading the Revolution* (Boston: Harvard Business School Press, 2000, pg. 15

[3] Burt Nanus, *Visionary Leadership.* San Francisco: Jossey-Bass Publishers, 1992, pg. 4.

[4] ibid, pg. xvii.

[5] Winston Churchill, *Churchill Speaks* (London: Chelsea House Publishers, 1980), pg. 713.

How to Read this Book

In Part I "Learning from the Past" we explore the history of American Manufacturing. We are on a trajectory toward the future. We intend to show that trajectory by a short review of our recent past.

In Chapter 1, titled **"The History of American Manufacturing– Where it All Came From"** we examine the impact of the First Industrial Revolution (from Manpower to Steam Power) and the Second Industrial Revolutions (of Modern Day Manufacturing Methods) on American Manufacturing.

In Chapter 2, which is called **"The Information Revolution in Manufacturing"**, we examine the impact of the Third Industrial Revolution that started after the 1940s and is still in process. In this chapter we explore the shift in manufacturing from Individuals to System Thinking, the growth of Lean and Six Sigma methodologies and the emergence of MRPII/ERP systems.

In Part Two, which is called **"Efficient and Profitable Customization"**, we take a look ahead to the future. We show how American manufacturing is only midway through these current trends and how these trends foreshadow the remaining topics in this book: systems thinking, the engineering pyramid, product configuration, configuration engineering and mass customization.

In Chapter 3, called **"It's Not about the Computer, it's about Systems Thinking"**, we explore how recent advances in Systems Thinking have helped to lower development costs.

In Chapter 4, called **"The Engineering Pyramid",** we introduce readers to our Engineering Pyramid paradigm and a top down approach that can be utilized to increase the speed of innovation and dramatically lower engineering costs.

In Chapter 5, called **"Systemization and Standardization – They are Not the Same"** we explore the current challenges of designing and building customized products and our methodology for top down systemization and standardization to increase the speed of innovation and dramatically lower engineering costs.

In Chapter 6, called **"Mass Customization"**, we demonstrate the importance of mass customization for the future of American manufacturing and describe how current leaders have made mass customization profitable in their businesses.

In Part Three, called **"The Human Component – It's Still All About the People"**, we look at the continuing importance and the necessity of people systems in the manufacturing process.

In Chapter 7, called **"Employee On Boarding"** we provide an approach to bringing people into the organization.

In Chapter 8, called **"High Performance Team-Based Work Systems "**, we tell you how to maximize throughput, profit and career rewards through an empowered team based work system..

In Chapter 9, called "**Technology Transfer and Training**", we explore how employees can learn the necessary skills for working in a highly efficient manufacturing environment.

The last section, Part Four, is entitled, "**Putting it All Together**". Here, in Chapter 10, called "**Taking Your Company There**" we tell you who will be the winners and losers of this natural extension of American manufacturers. Also, we tell you how you will know if it's too late for your company. Sorry…some of you readers won't be happy.

Part One
Learning from the Past

Chapter 1
The History of American Manufacturing

Key Concepts:

- Prior to the First Industrial Revolution, manufacturing was predominately the craftsman's workshop
- After the First Industrial Revolution, manufacturing became the inventor's workshop
- After the Second Industrial Revolution, manufacturing became the capitalists workshop

To understand where manufacturing is currently and where it is going it is helpful to look first at the origins of American manufacturing.

Manufacturing Before the First Industrial Revolution

Manufacturing before the First Industrial Revolution remained substantially unchanged for 1,000s of years.

The process before the First Industrial Revolution (in the late 1700's), was that individual craftsmen created products for individual clients.

Early American craftsmen were silversmiths, tanners, carpenters and stone masons.

During the period prior to the First Industrial Revolution, the product idea, design, and manufacturing were all performed by a single individual with the assistance of apprentices and other lower skilled individuals.

The size of the manufacturing enterprise was limited to the craftsman's ability to: collect the necessary capital to create the workshop, oversee all aspects of the operations in his workshop, and to effectively distribute his product.

First Industrial Revolution

Starting in the late 1700s, the First Industrial Revolution ushered in many inventions.

One major invention during this period was the steam engine. The steam engine created previously unheard of amounts of concentrated energy which was soon harnessed to manufacture and distribute on a massive scale. This allowed for mass consumption of mass produced products.

The First Industrial Revolution, which was the *workshop of the inventor*, laid some important groundwork for the Second Industrial Revolution. First, manufacturing enterprises became too large to become operated by a team of generalists. The modern functional organization was born where work was divided between: marketing, design, manufacturing, sales, and distribution.

Second, the capital required to lay railroads, on the scale required gave birth to the legal entity of the corporation, where large numbers of anonymous investors could receive the shared benefits of their investments without the commensurate liability.

In all recorded history before this time, the craftsman received all the benefits and liabilities of his own efforts. With a separation between the investor and the liabilities of the corporation; the stock market allowed large amounts of capital to be amassed, not just for railroads, but also for other projects.

Second Industrial Revolution

The Second Industrial Revolution (in the late 1800's) brought together many natural consequences of the first industrial revolution. Two of these concepts are very important for the future of American manufacturing.

First, the concept of economies of scale was discovered as many pre-industrial revolution businesses were replaced by businesses with enough capital to realize economies of scale in each given industry.

Second, the concept of interchangeable parts was created as an outgrowth of the Civil War for manufacturing guns. Interchangeable parts made mass production much more efficient and ushered in numerous innovations: electricity, agricultural equipment, the automobile, the airplane, and the telephone.

It is important to note that after the Second Industrial Revolution, manufacturing (and farming) was no longer a cottage industry. Manufacturing became the workshop for those who were able to pull together the necessary capital to create new infrastructures.

After the Second Industrial Revolution, Manufacturing became the workshop for those who were able to pull together the necessary capital to create new infrastructures.

Notes

[1] Al Chandler, "The Invisible Hand".

Chapter 2
The Start of the Third Revolution

Key Concepts:

- Building Blocks to the Third Revolution
- xRP

The Third Industrial Revolution

After the First Industrial Revolution (of the late 1700s) and the Second Industrial Revolution (of the late 1800s), a Third Industrial Revolution emerged in the 1940s.

This Third Industrial Revolution started in the 1940s, but it is only halfway to its natural conclusion. What started in the 1940s was the invention of the digital computer, and its emerging application to manufacturing challenges.

This book is about where this Third Revolution is going. We used to think the Third Revolution was only about computerization or digitalization, and early advances in this revolution were indeed about computerization. But, the First Industrial Revolution was about much more than steam: it was about the previously unforeseen logical consequences that steam power introduced: mass production, mass distribution, mass marketing, etc.

Similarly, this Third Revolution is about much more than computerization: it is about what many have not seen yet, the logical consequences that computerization introduces. But before we discuss the logical conclusions of the Third Revolution in the next chapters, we want to do two things in this chapter. First, let's look at the building blocks we now have; and second, let's assess our current situation at the halfway point in this Third Industrial Revolution.

The Third Revolution is about much more than computerization: it is about what many have not seen yet, the logical consequences that computerization introduces.

Just like a house is more than bricks; so, the vision we are discussing is more than computer-age building blocks. At the same time, to build our house, we need to clearly understand what these blocks are and what they enable. So, let's take a look at the computer-age building blocks that now service the half-evolved future manufacturing enterprise.

Mass Communication

The information age has shrunk the world. Though this is not the end result, let's look at this current situation:

- The mass market now extends beyond any single nation, to the world. Consumers all over the world can be listened to and promised products that meet their individual and local needs.

- The World Consumer knows what products are being produced for other members of the world community, and now wants these products for themselves, according to their own unique situation.

- The World Producer knows what products are being demanded, and knows whether they have value-added which can make a superior product in terms of cost or features. This is true for all product components, so the end products being produced are cheaper and better than those that were produced in previous regional markets.

CAD/CAM

At the halfway point, we also have the Computer Aided Design (CAD) and Computer Aided Manufacturing (CAM) building blocks. But what we have is more than the ability to use computers to make part drawings (CAD), or the use of computer descriptions of parts to automatically manufacture those parts (CAM). What we have now is a way for computers to communicate about products in ways that are understandable by humans and manufacturable by automated machinery. So we can communicate on a mass scale about yet to be realized products, and product concepts using the CAD/CAM building block.

Manufacturing Information Systems

When the digital computer was first introduced in manufacturing, it was first used to automate accounting functions. Soon thereafter, it was realized that the computer could be used to make sure all the inventories needed for production were on-hand or on order, this was called Materials Requirements Planning (MRP). The need for MRP systems created the original industry using computers to solve problems that were unique to manufacturing. MRP soon gave way to what was called MRP II, "Manufacturing Resource Planning," where all related activities in the manufacturing enterprise were computerized: forecasting, financial management modules, capacity requirement planning, purchasing, inventory management, scheduling and other modules. This then eventually gave way to the current version of these systems, ERP, "Enterprise Resource Planning," where all aspects of any business enterprise are computerized.

As MRP/ERP systems evolved to support manufacturing business functions, the use of computers on the shop floor also evolved. Shop Floor Control systems were introduced to provide print-outs of what was supposed to be done on a given day, and to document these accomplishments. These systems have evolved to what is today called a Manufacturing Execution System (MES), which is an on-line system for continuously monitoring the status of production, and using this status to direct immediate activities.

Also, in the process industries (refineries, chemical plants, power plants, food processing, etc.), computers were used to directly control individual processes in Distributed Control Systems (DCS), and computers were used to set up control rooms for status reporting and controlling the whole factory, called Supervisory Controls and Data Acquisition Systems (SCADA).

Visibility and Modern Quality Management

The computer also allowed factory managers to track all of the activities in their plants, so they could analyze the effectiveness of their processes and improve them. Computerized factories allowed for the invention of various productivity initiatives. This included the Lean Manufacturing concept, where all waste is made clearly visible and tagged for elimination. It also included Total Quality Management and Six Sigma concepts where statistically significant data about the manufacturer's processes can be collected and analyzed to optimize these processes and minimize their variability. Visibility of what is going on in the factory also allowed factory managers, factory workers, other managers and customers to know exactly what is going on with their products.

Computer Architecture

There have also been trends in computer architecture, which support all of these individual uses of computing in manufacturing. Early CAD/CAM, MRP, MRP II, and SCADA systems all depended on a single centralized computer, where users either logged in through a terminal, responded to printed reports, or supplied information to be entered into the system.

Current ERP and CAD/CAM systems use a client-server computing model, where data is stored on the server; but computing is done locally at the user's computer.

But, this is not the end. Recent advances in computing paint a picture of fully distributed intelligent computer systems supporting the world-wide manufacturing enterprise, in what has been called a massively distributed multi-agent architecture. In this computing paradigm end consumers, intermediate consumers, and all productive capabilities can all be connected together through a world-wide web of computing agents that represent their needs and capabilities to each other through standard languages for describing and globally optimizing these needs and capabilities. Image a customer orders widgets from a company, the agent for the widget communicates with agents representing each step in the widget manufacturing process, agents representing raw material suppliers and agents representing all external suppliers. A three-dimensional quote is returned to the customer in real-time displaying the delivery function for that widget that the supply chain can deliver. Simply put, being able to make commitments to customers that the supply chain can keep while being more responsive to your customer.

Where This is All Headed

The logical conclusion of all these pieces is what we call xRP, the web-based resource planning and consumer satisfying computer-age building block that is now possible. To be clear, this is still just a building block. The next chapters are about what can be built with these building blocks, and how to put these blocks together. xRP is the inevitable computer-age building block which connects all consumers, to all producers, in a proactive fashion, so that all needs are known, all capabilities are utilized, and all questions about how those needs are being met are immediately available. This is built on mass communication capabilities; where potential and actual products are described in ways that consumers and producers both understand; where resource planning and consumer desires are optimized against those needs; and where all stages of production are visible to the consumer, including internal organizations, to assure that what is being produced conforms to all requirements.

So given the xRP building block, how do we use this new steam engine to create the future of American manufacturing? That's what the next chapters are about.

xRP is the inevitable computer-age building block which connects all consumers, to all producers, in a proactive fashion, so that all needs are known, all capabilities are utilized, and all questions about how those needs are being met are immediately available.

Part Two
Efficient and Profitable
Customization

Chapter 3
It's Not about the Computer It's about Systems Thinking

Key Concepts:

- System Thinking
- Lowering Costs
- Product Customization

For most engineers it is much easier and thought provoking to start from scratch each time that they begin something. Most engineers are taught the basics in colleges therefore they are most comfortable starting with the basics.

Building a system from pre-existing knowledge is perceived to be riskier. Why? Because of:

- dependency on other peoples work
- lack of understanding of the constraints on the work
- minimizing individual creativity

The solution, therefore is not to "Reinvent the Wheel" but to use the wheel over and over again.

To "use the wheel over and over again", it is necessary to constrain the environment in which the engineer can become creative. In other words, engineers can innovate, but not from a "blank sheet of paper". They innovate within known boundaries or constraints.

One example of how engineers can do this effectively was displayed by the "Apollo 13" mission.

The mission for the engineers was to save the astronauts who were trapped in their spacecraft, adrift in space. The engineers on the ground were constrained by what the astronauts had on board. And they were successful in getting the crew successfully back to earth.

In a similar fashion, we have seen engineers work successfully, within known boundaries and constraints.

We have seen three typical approaches to engineering:

- Engineers who have been given no direction and work from "a clean sheet of paper". This will nearly always cost the enterprise profit.

- Engineers who have been given direction and work from "a clean sheet of paper". This approach we have seen will allow the enterprise to break even at best.

- Engineers who have been given direction and constraints. This approach will contribute to the company's bottom line.

The work with constraints, knowledge and hardware need to be presented to engineers in a way to make them comfortable and personally rewarded for working within the system and using the system over and over again.

To do this it will be important to:

1. Design systems with not a specific end in mind but a range of the end.

   It is far harder to predict the product that will win versus a range of products that could win. Use the same line of thinking in designing your manufacturing system. Remember-How the consumer sees your product is what SELLS the product.

2. Use an approach that defines common components within the range. It simplifies all aspects of the product and manufacturing system.

The remaining portion of this chapter identifies additional steps that are necessary for product customization.

How the consumer sees your product is what SELLS the product.

Product Customization

Due to customer needs, made-to-order customized products will soon become the norm. "Demand for more customized goods will transform manufacturing by creating shorter product life cycles, and thus shorter production runs. Batches of identical products will become smaller as consumers increasingly demand differentiated offerings and marketers respond to information about customers with increased segmentation and customization [1]."

Manufacturers increasingly need to look for ways to optimize their current sales process and information systems for made-to-order products.

Current Problems with Product Customization

Currently, companies face many challenges in attempting to customize products for specific customer needs. These issues include:

Engineering Issues

- ❑ Slow cycle time and inefficiency when engineering custom orders
- ❑ Imperfect translation of customer requirements
- ❑ Slow delivery in design of deliverables

Sales and Marketing Issues

- ❑ Delays in turnaround on requests for proposals
- ❑ Delays in getting feedback from customers
- ❑ Inaccuracy in meeting customer requirements

Manufacturing Issues

- ❑ Inability to accurately predict product shipment
- ❑ Long-lead times from poor systemization of the custom manufacturing process
- ❑ Inability to realize the cost savings possible from the direct-to-customer, custom manufacturing model

- ❏ Delays and inaccuracy in creating designs and drawings

- ❏ Rework and scrap on custom orders

Corporate Issues

- ❏ Inability to realize expected increases in:
  - o Revenue
  - o Market Share
  - o Profitability
  - o Customer Loyalty

Current Custom Manufacturing Work Processes

Currently, for a product to be customized, there are a number of interactions that take place between the customer, sales force, engineers and manufacturers.

Custom Manufacturing

Work Process

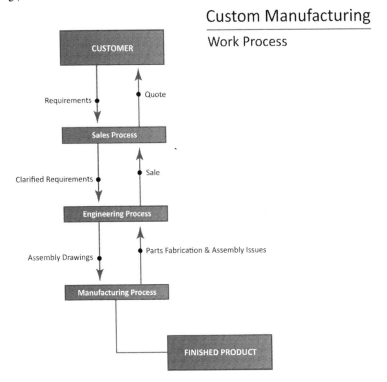

These interactions include: account representatives receiving customer requirements, providing quotes, clarifying requirements with engineers, creating assembly drawings, and providing solutions for assembly issues before creating a customized finished product.

Interactions in the custom manufacturing work process currently can take a great deal of time and can be very labor intensive. In addition, the knowledge required to meet the customer's needs, from the sales process through the manufacturing process, is typically stored in the heads of various people within the organization.

Current Sales Process

The time and effort required to develop a request for a quote can be staggering, and the quote may not even lead to a sale.

The process usually involves a sales contact, a team of engineers, the manufacturing organization, and the heads of the company. The cost and time per quote can be extensive depending on the complexity of the product. The losses from this sales process are not only reflected in the cost but also in the amount of time required by highly skilled people who could be supporting other aspects of building the business.

Much of the knowledge in the current sales process resides in different experts within the company and is not integrated and accessible to the sales representatives and eventually to the customer. After the sale is made, resources need to be focused at determining the real customer requirements. Many times information discussed in the sales process is unclear or missed. The resulting quote may have to be adjusted or margins compromised to keep a customer satisfied.

Sales Process

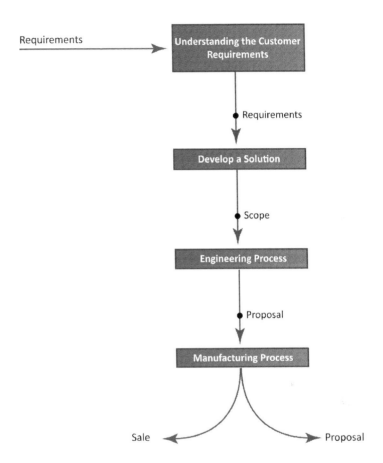

Current Engineering Work Process

In the engineering process, the customer's needs are captured in the engineering drawings and documents.

Once this is complete, the fabrication, procurement, and assembly of the product begins. The knowledge of what to purchase resides in the procurement organization that may find long lead times, delays or problems with availability of the parts resulting in reengineering the assemblies with different parts.

Engineering
Work Process

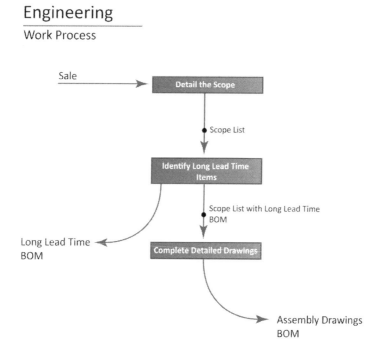

Current Manufacturing Work Process

Once the parts are released to manufacturing for fabrication, part tolerances may not be clear leading to some parts being unable to be assembled. The subassembly process may require special knowledge because of the custom nature of the assemblies.

Custom Manufacturing Work Process

Configurable System

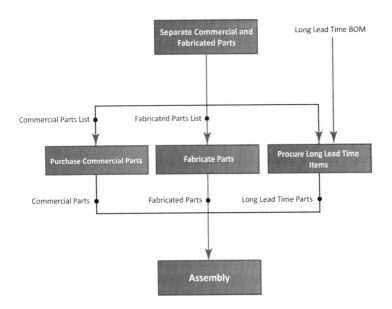

In summary, the process can require much rework and cost both time and money to your organization and the customer.

A product configuration system can be useful to manage this level of complexity. Developing a product configuration system involves the identification of standard parts subassemblies and processes that can be configured to meet customer needs. These standard parts subassemblies and processes are engineered to meet a wide range of customer needs.

Product configurators allow for the dynamic configuration of complex products (meaning that many products can be made available with numerous interdependent options).

Utilizing a product configuration system drastically reduces the time involved in selling, designing, and manufacturing custom ordered parts, assemblies, or finished products by intelligently identifying the physical attributes of a manufactured item and utilizing specific parameters to generate engineering and manufacturing deliverables.

Configurable Custom Manufacturing Work Process

With a configurable model, automation reduces the number of interactions that take place between the customer, sales force, engineers and manufacturers.

Custom Manufacturing Work Process

Configurable System

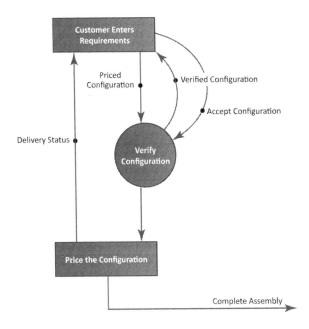

Configuration Process

The Configuration Process in a configurable system uses software applications to allow the customer to enter specific requirements. However, customer options are limited to specific parameters based on company standards.

Configuration Process
Configurable System

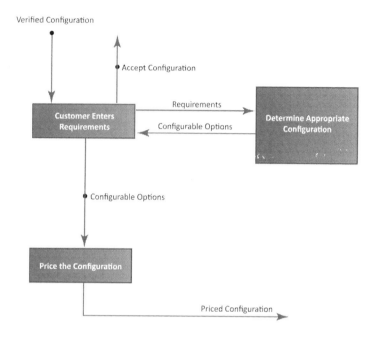

Configurable Manufacturing Process

Using configurable products, the manufacturing process becomes much different than current made-to-order product manufacturing.

In a configurable system, ordering for parts is automated, making it clear which parts need to be fabricated and which need to be purchased through a commercial vendor.

Custom Manufacturing Work Process

Configuration System

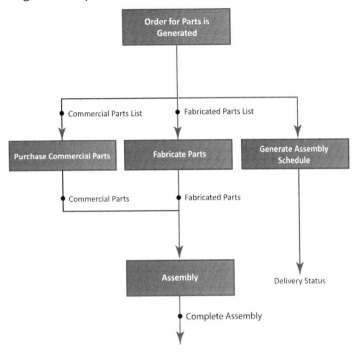

Challenges to Using a Configurable System

It takes some forethought and work to determine the functional requirements for each part and subassembly in a configurable system.

The structures need to be defined in a way that parameters are defined and the parts can change to meet the varying requirements.

The discipline to stay within constraints of the configurable parts is essential to making money with configuration engineering.

Engineers, by nature, want to create a much-improved solution to meet each specific customer requirement.

This effort often leads to highly specialized solutions that are more expensive and difficult to manufacture, requiring a great deal of new learning in the fabrication and assembly process. Establishing the critical few standard components and only customizing where unique value can be added is the key to successfully win in a highly competitive market.

As manufacturers look for ways to optimize their existing processes for made-to-order products, establishing the critical few standard components and only customizing where unique value can be added is the key to win in a highly competitive market.

As manufacturers look for ways to optimize their existing processes for made-to-order products establishing the critical few standard components and only customizing where unique value can be added is the key to successfully win in a highly competitive market.

The next chapter provides even greater detail on how to leverage product configuration with a top-down approach to achieve true configuration engineering. We've named this methodology, "The Engineering Pyramid".

Notes

[1] *Made To Order*, 1 to 1 Magazine, October 2001.

Chapter 4
The Engineering Pyramid

Key Concepts:

- The Top Down Approach
- Increasing Innovation Speed
- Lowering Engineering Costs

Engineering Productivity Pyramid

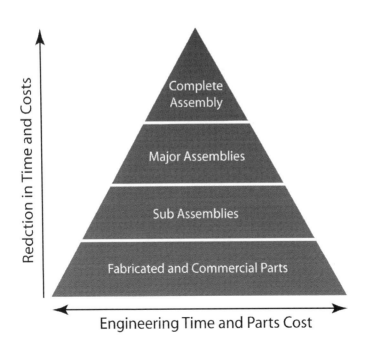

The Model

The Engineering Pyramid is a methodology that we have created to identify how organizations can increase innovation speed and lower engineering costs.

It is needed because there are pressures on an organization to deliver custom designs to meet specific needs and to reduce the cost to deliver varying designs.

The Engineering Pyramid Methodology

- Take advantage of the parts and assemblies that already have most of the common components and use them as the basis of the next machine

- Parts and assemblies must be designed to support reuse in many applications

- Engineers need to pay attention on how assemblies are structured and the interfaces to these assemblies to get them to be reused

- Develop the system from the top-down

How to implement
The Engineering Pyramid:

A. Develop the system from a top-down approach.

1. Functionally describe what you are building on the top-level before executing the design.

2. Begin with a top-down approach by defining the highest level assembly before defining lower level assemblies.

3. Work your way down to the detail level making sure all constraints at the upper level are being followed.

4. Design the interfaces in a common format between functions

B. Use a documentation system that flows from top down. (In most engineering systems documentation flows from the bottom up.)

1. Connect all information to the entity/part.

2. Document in a way that if the higher assembly is reused, all the information travels with it.

3. Establish relationships from the assemblies that flow from the top down.

4. Allow users to drill down into the level of detail they need.

5. Create views of the information for different users

Example:

A person that operates the equipment needs a different level of information than a person that maintains the equipment.

C. Leverage the Engineering Pyramid

    1.   Train on:
        a.   Design for re-use
        b.   Leveraging component interfaces
        c.   Design using the top-down approach

    2.   Reward people for re-application of existing components.

    3.   Reap Profitable Innovation

Leveraging the Engineering Pyramid:

Our approach will lead to:

- Less development and rework due to elimination of unique designs

- Faster deliver of products to the customer

- Lower engineering costs

Those who adapt this methodology will be the low cost, fast producer for their industry.

Chapter 5
Systemization and Standardization
(They are Not the Same)

Key Concepts:

- Product Standardization
- Product Systemization

The Issue

Systemization and standardization are two of the keys to making manufacturing work.

Systemization is the process of defining what range of products will be made and what range of production processes will be employed. Standardization is the process of defining what specific products will be made and what specific production techniques will be used to make these products.

As demand for customized products increases, new product designs proliferate, frequently using different designs for similar functions. These new designs, although designed to meet customer demands, can create numerous inefficiencies such as: increased operating costs, complexity in procurement and communication and a decrease in delivery speed.

Without product standardization, manufacturers will see increases in costs for their made-to-order goods.

Without product systemization, manufacturers will see increases in costs for their made-to-order goods.

By overly constraining the products and production processes, manufacturers will increasingly find their products irrelevant to the world marketplace.

To systemize:

a. Develop a system to support each and every function

b. The system needs to be adaptable or customized for the need

c. A system with a lot of checklists that do not apply to the application will fall to the wayside

d. The system needs to benefit the user, customer and company

Standardize on parts that have multiuse or a range of use: For example, in converting there are components for web handling such as nip rolls, S-wraps and idlers and there is equipment to unwind and rewind these webs.

    i. Ex: Nip rolls can also be designed to do an S-Wrap function
    ii. Ex: Unwinds can be designed to do rewind
    iii. Ex. A standard width idler can be used in a variety of idler applications

The remaining portion of this chapter looks at even greater detail of the steps for systemization.

Current Problems __Without__ Product Systemization

Currently, companies face many challenges if they do not rigorously systemize their products. These challenges include:

Engineering Issues

❑ Slow delivery in design of deliverables
(Many engineering hours in engineering different subcomponents)

❑ Slow cycle time and inefficiency when engineering custom orders

Sales and Marketing Issues

❑ Delays in turnaround on requests for proposals

Manufacturing Issues

❑ Delays and inaccuracy in creating designs and drawings

Corporate Issues

❑ Increased Operating Costs

❑ Decreased Profitability

What is Product Systemization?

Product systemization is the process of eliminating redundant products, platforms and processes and systematizing these elements into a defined structure for future growth and cost reduction.

Systemization focuses on using standard parts and part derivatives in "same function" applications.

When systemization occurs, product offerings (sometimes referred to as Stock Keeping Units or SKUs) are typically eliminated and systematized for greater efficiency, unless these additional SKUs are seen as value add by the customer.

This is especially important in product categories where customers focus principally on price. If one product is relatively the same as another, offering multiple SKUs will not be that important to the consumer and will be a poor source of revenue.

When systemization occurs, platforms are also eliminated and systematized for greater efficiency. Prior to systemization, many manufacturers find themselves maintaining multiple platforms because of their different product offerings, acquisitions or because of the selective implementation of new technology. Eliminating multiple platforms can result in dramatic cost savings in operating *expenses*.

Years ago, a large consumer products company eliminated 13 of its 14 global manufacturing platforms, deciding that all of its global production facilities will use one standard platform. The company realized a cost savings of 500 million dollars over the next five years.

What are the Benefits to Product Systemization?

Product systemization offers a number of benefits for organizations:

- operating cost reduction
- faster product delivery
- increased profitability.

Storeroom Cost Reductions

Organizations can expect significant savings in operating costs after systemizing their products where the only part variety supported is part variety that brings value to the customer. With the reduction of inventory, storeroom costs (the inventory carrying costs for an item) are greatly reduced. Storeroom costs for an item tend to be approximately twenty five percent of the value of the item per year, due to taxes and storeroom operation costs. In reducing inventory, this cost savings can be realized.

Product Supplier Cost Reductions

Another operating cost reduction that many companies find is in leveraging economies of scale. Instead of ordering many different parts, the process of product systemization creates the opportunity for a company to order large quantities of only a few types of parts. This can lead to significant savings from vendors.

Engineering Cost Reductions

Another important, yet frequently overlooked, savings regarding product systemization is the reduction of engineering costs. After an organization systemizes their products, platforms and processes, engineers do not have to focus on new system design and development. This means that new and relatively inexperienced engineers can be utilized because they are given a template to follow with defined standards in place. Engineers can then focus on productivity instead of designing a new system for each new product. This savings in engineering time can be a reduction of 25-50% of your engineering staff, if not more.

Increased Delivery Speed

Another important benefit to systemizing products is in the reduction of production and delivery time. Product systemization allows for time to be saved throughout the sales, engineering, manufacturing and fulfillment. Using a standard template, engineers can quickly add products to existing platforms. This increased delivery speed will increase the utilization of engineers and allow for quicker delivery time for your customers.

Systemization Considerations

There are several items that must be considered prior to implementing a product systemization program. These areas include considering your organization's usage of commercial parts, fabricated parts and standard assemblies/subassemblies.

Commercial Parts

When utilizing commercial parts in a product systemization program, there are several considerations to keep in mind.

1. One must first determine if the product is available in the *global market*. If a commercial part is to be used on platforms globally, the commercial part must be readily available from a reliable vendor.

2. A second consideration in product systemization is to understand the *stability* of the commercial part. If the part has a record of changing frequently, the systemization process will not have the desired affect. It is critical that a commercial part be stable, in order to work within a systemized process.

3. Another consideration is *price*. Consider the multiple-use of a commercial part from a single vendor with a proven track record. Even though the vendor may not offer the cheapest price on a one-up part, the vendor may payout because of purchase of a large quantity over a longer period of time.

4. Another consideration is the *breadth of application* a part can be used in. A part with a broader range of

flexibility will last longer than a part with narrow application potential.

5. Another consideration is asking, *"What does the customer use?"* Parts and vendors that *are widely used by your customer base* will be more accepted. For example, if most of your customer base use Allen Bradley, then standardizing on Allen Bradley will be more readily accepted.

6. Identify commercial parts that are more *configurable* and which have a broader use within the product lines. These parts will be essential for customizing products.

Fabricated Parts

Unlike manufactured parts, considerations when working with fabricated parts in product systemization have more to do with machining and assembly complexity than price and availability. Establishing standards around the use of parts will go hand in hand with systemizing fabricated assemblies. If common parameters are determined for all of the applications, fabricated parts can be designed and used over and over again. For example, if dimensions fit within standard parameters, fabricated parts can be used over and over again on a machine.

Once a standard is established for a set of fabricated parts, each one can be optimized to reduce costs in the fabrication process. One example is conveyors on a converting line.

One manufacturer recently went from individually engineered conveyers to a single design with a modified vacuum plate design for different product line widths. With this systemization in place, the cost of conveyers was cut in half.

Standard Assemblies/Sub Assemblies

The ability to develop standards for upper level assemblies opens the door for configuration engineering and a reduction in assembly cost. This area is by far the most complicated. Each product and product line needs to identify common product structures and the parameters that differentiate the product lines and their derivatives. This level is the most constraining of the systemization process. It requires a great deal of system thinking and top down design skill.

SKUs and Product Categories

Before cutting Stock Keeping Units (SKUs), it is imperative to carefully look at the product categories in which you sell. In premium categories, for example SKUs should be trimmed very cautiously. Because there is typically high customer loyalty for these highly innovative SKUs in premium categories (such as premium breakfast cereals or analgesics) SKU proliferation "tends to be a good thing despite the cost." [2]. Tylenol, for example, "comes in regular, extra strength, and children's dosages; in normal and extended relief; in tablets, caplets, gelcaps, geltabs, and as a liquid; in combination with other over-the-counter medications; in packages that are child-proof and, for arthritis-suffers, in packages that are extra easy to open-all of these and more in a variety of sizes." [3]

Altogether, Tylenol is sold in at least seventy SKUs. In measuring sales, Tylenol's historic annual growth rate is "clear evidence that consumers take a positive view of this level of choice and variety." [4].

For non-premium product categories, SKU reduction makes good sense. In product categories where customers focus principally on price, one product is relatively the same as another, thus offering multiple SKUs will not be that important to the consumer and will be a poor source of revenue.

In summary, the product systemization process can require a great deal of planning and review of considerations such as the utilization of commercial parts, fabricated parts, standard assemblies/subassemblies and product category.

Product Systemization Checklist

As your organization considers product systemization, use this checklist to help strategize and plan:

1. *Identify all components.* Identify the part/part family or products/product family that currently exist. Identify how they are used and the feature and/or benefit of using the component.

2. *Justify the existence* of all components.

3. *Identify all redundant components.*

4. *Eliminate all redundant components.* Rigorously drop all components that are duplicated.

5. *Justify the existence of all components* using only one product family.

6. *Determine assemblies and sub-assemblies* from justified parts.

7. Eliminate or at least create a plan to *eliminate assemblies/sub-assemblies* with redundant functionality (if possible).

8. *Design engineering strategies.*

9. *Determine price breaks* from the product's supplier. For example, identify quantity discounts if a large quantity of one part is ordered, versus many smaller orders for many separate components.

Challenges to Implementing Product Systemization

It takes some forethought and work to determine the functional requirements for each part and subassembly in a systemized process.

The structures need to be defined in a way that parameters are defined and the parts can change to meet the varying requirements. A discipline to stay within constraints of the systemized products is essential to making money with systemized engineering.

Engineers by nature want to create a much-improved solution to meet each specific customer requirement. This effort often leads to highly specialized solutions that are more expensive and difficult to manufacture and require a great deal of new learning in the fabrication and assembly process. Establishing the critical few standard components and only allowing variety where unique value can be added is the key to win in a highly competitive market.

Establishing the critical few standard components and only allowing variety where unique value can be added is the key to win in a highly competitive market.

Notes

[1] *Institute for the Future and Peppers & Rogers Group*, Consumer Research Report, 2001.

[2] *The Complexity of Reducing Complexity*, Vijay Vishwanath and Jonathan Mark, Bain Strategy Brief, 1997.

[3] ibid

[4] ibid

Chapter 6
Mass Customization

Key Concepts:

- What is Mass Customization
- How to Mass Customize

"The mass-customization of a product, if it's done right, represents an almost air-tight guarantee of a satisfied, loyal, long-term customer. ... Mass-customization is the ultimate form of customer differentiation."

D. Peppers & M. Rogers
The One to One Future,
(Doubleday,1993)

"The more a company can deliver customized goods on a mass basis, relative to their competition, the greater is their competitive advantage."

S. Davis
Future Perfect, (Addison-Wesley, 1987)

What is Mass Customization?

Mass customization aims to provide goods and services that meet individual customers' requirements with near mass production efficiency.

For over a decade, futurists have said that mass customized goods and services are the future for our economy. These predictions seemed off the mark for most of the past decade, until towards the end of the decade, it became obvious that Dell Computer Corporation had used this paradigm to go from a negligible market share to market dominance in the PC industry.

Other companies experimented with the paradigm: Nike athletic shoes; Mattel toys; CDNow CDs; P&G cosmetics and coffee; GM, Ford, Saturn and Nissan with automobiles; Levi's and Brooks Brothers with apparel; and a host of small startups making products as varied as custom athletic equipment, custom nutritional supplements, custom bicycles, and custom lighting systems.

Why Mass Customize?

The mass customization value proposition comes from the dual opportunities of increased market share and higher profit margins.

Market Share:

Mass customization can result in increased market share:

- by satisfying the customer with the exact product they want;

- by meeting customer pull for custom made products;

- by offering a product which is differentiated from other products through being specifically made for each individual;

- by being able to quickly spot market trends;

- by creating high switching costs for the customer through having established knowledge of their exact preferences, measurements, or lifestyle;

- by being able to use that relationship to add related businesses.

Profit Margins:

The mass customizer receives higher profit margins:

- by being able to charge higher prices;

- by increasing inventory turns;

- by eliminating finished goods inventory;

- by eliminating the chance of inventory obsolescence;

- by freeing up working capital through manufacturing faster than suppliers expect payment and receiving payment from consumers upon shipping the order;

- by eliminating distribution channels and selling custom products directly to the customer;

- by getting the consumer to trade up to higher margin features;

- by using the direct relationship with the customer to add high margin businesses.

The Power of Mass Customization

Increased Market Share

- strong customer pull
- Internet drawing card
- ultimate in differentiation
- direct customer relationship
- high switching costs
- adding related businesses
- new sales channels (e.g. Internet)

Higher Profit Margins

- higher prices
- no obsolescence or markdowns
- dis-intermediation
- increased inventory turns
- no finished good inventory
- excess working capital
- high-margin features
- add high-margin businesses

How to Mass Customize?

These phenomenal benefits are not obtained by incremental changes to a mass production system, but by a fundamental switch in production paradigms. Our advice for making the change is:

1) Start small. As systems and techniques are proven, scale them up.

2) Start at the front end of the production processes first, use shallow customization there, and as the mass customization systems are proven, backwards integrate into the parts of the mass production systems which will provide the greatest consumer value by being made flexible.

3) Use software systems designed to support this new paradigm, don't expect that mass production software can be made to fit this new paradigm with only minor modifications.

4) Make the above stated benefits of mass customization the goals of the mass customization project. As the mass customization project is being planned and deployed, check the project against these goals.

Mass Customization Quotes

"A business can charge more if consumers think its product is differentiated from others. Obviously, the most differentiated product is something designed specifically for one customer."

J. William Gurley
Fortune, Oct 12, 1998

"The economic logic behind the mass-customization of products is, today, as inevitable and irresistible as the logic of the assembly line was at the beginning of the century. It is not a question of *whether* this kind of manufacturing process will take over— only of *when* it will happen"

D. Peppers & M. Rogers
The One to One Future,
(Doubleday, 1993)

Mass Customization Terminology

- **Customer Sacrifice Gap** – the gap between the product the customer wants and what is available in the market

- **Good Variety vs. Bad Variety** – good variety is product/service variety that customers are willing to pay additional for. Bad variety is variety that customers are not willing to pay for.

- **4 Faces of Mass Customization**

    - **Transparent** – providing customers with customized products whose customization is transparent or unknown by the end user

    - **Collaborative** – customers collaborate with customizer on the design and delivery of the product to specifically meet the customer's needs

    - **Adaptive** – providing a standardized product that is able to be customized in the hands of the end user

    - **Cosmetic** – providing a standardized product that is marketed to different customer groups in unique ways

- **Deep vs. Shallow Customization** – providing a low level of customization versus a deep level of customization that may change product appearance and performance

Pine's 4 Faces of Mass Customization

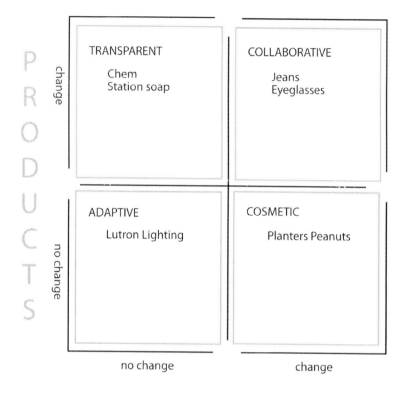

PRODUCTS

change

TRANSPARENT

Chem
Station soap

COLLABORATIVE

Jeans
Eyeglasses

no change

ADAPTIVE

Lutron Lighting

COSMETIC

Planters Peanuts

no change

change

representation

Source: Pine & Gilmore

Types of Mass Customized Product

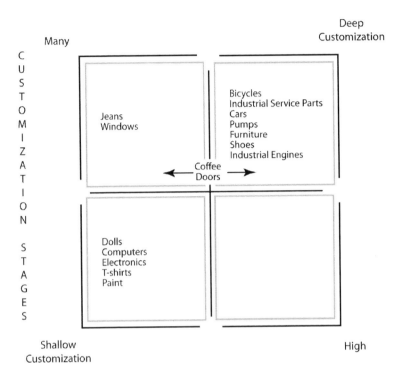

Deep Customization

Many

C
U
S
T
O
M
I
Z
A
T
I
O
N

S
T
A
G
E
S

Jeans
Windows

Bicycles
Industrial Service Parts
Cars
Pumps
Furniture
Shoes
Industrial Engines

Coffee
Doors

Dolls
Computers
Electronics
T-shirts
Paint

Shallow
Customization

High

Process Variety at Each Stage

Standard Wisdom for Custom Manufacturing Processes

- Systematize the Product
  - **Dell's product modularization**

    Dell modularized their production system to quickly manufacture personal computers for individual customers.

  - **GE's Part Recognition Code**

    GE Service Parts won Society of Manufacturing Engineers' LEAD Award for the Part Recognition Code concept and supporting systems. The Part Code consisted of Four Elements (Part Family, Shape Substructures, Gross Properties and Dimensional and Notational Data) and was variable length.

    E.g. BLT-12-AFCCADNE-L4,L5,L9,L10,D13,A1,A2,A3,R1,R2

    This part code traveled with the part and allowed for support systems like sales, customer service, engineering, process planning, scheduling, etc. to use this detailed part code.

- Postpone Customization
  - shallow customization is preferred to deep customization
  - e.g. HP's Printers Customized at Distribution Center

- Modularize the Manufacturing Processes
  - easier to distribute production
  - easier to add new product features
  - fits with the modularity of the product

- Job-Shop / Single-Process / Cellular Production Facility fed by Kanban based inventory buffers

- Be Careful of Using Off-the-Shelf Software to Support New Business Model. Off-the-Shelf software is generally built for mass production and NOT mass customization.

Mass Production vs. Mass Customization

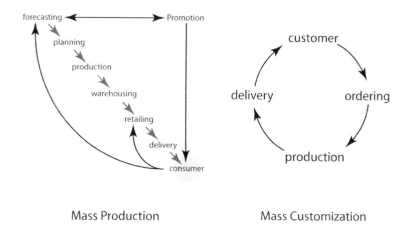

Mass Production   Mass Customization

Requirements for Mass Customization

- Wide Product Variety

- Short Lead-Times

- Consumer Feels Like Directly Interacting with Factory
    - customer-centric instead of production-centric
    - product features play off vs. manufacturing capability
    - scheduling production
    - notifications of key production milestones
    - watch product being made

- Flexible Automation Technologies where Appropriate

- Integrated with Modern IT Capabilities
- Modular and Easy to Reconfigure / Distribute

- Cost Effective

Steps to Mass Customization

- Determine Product Offering
  - Marketing, Engineering, Manufacturing

- Implement Systems
  - Web Page / Call Centers / Sales Systems
  - Product Design / Test
  - Manufacturing Systems (plant, equipment, IT)

- Ongoing Operation
  - Obtain Customer Feedback
    - modify product
    - improve service
  - Optimize Production Processes

Notes

[1] Markets of One: Creating Customer-Unique Value through Mass Customization, Gilmore & Pine, 2000.

Part Three
The Human Component – It's Still All About the People

Chapter 7
Employee On Boarding

Key Concepts:

- Creating the Right First Impression with Employees
- Holding Other Employees Accountable for New Employees

Welcoming, Embracing, Mentoring, Training and Retaining Employees

The future factory will still depend on people. It will produce products for individuals, and it will be run by individuals. Given that we are painting a unique vision of manufacturing, it is essential that all employees understand and embrace the new vision.

There is no more effective way to convey to new employees what the Values and Principles of an organization are than to have them demonstrated first by top management. At a minimum, the top executive(s) for the respective facility should make themselves available for whatever amount of time necessary to adequately allow for interactive discussion with new employees. This is an excellent opportunity to also discuss in detail the Corporate Mission Statement, Goals and overall Policy.

This discussion will be greatly enhanced through the use of multimedia tools (PowerPoint Slides, Acrobat, etc.) and should incorporate a minimal number of charts and graphs.

However, the use of digital photos of other employees, facilities and products tends to create a more personalized connection. It is also suggested that "hand-outs" be kept to a minimum. This enables the facilitator(s) to maintain group interaction with a minimum of distraction. It is extremely important that facilitators are open and honest as this is the first impression that the new employees will get regarding the company. **It will be a lasting one!**

This "On Boarding" concept is designed to facilitate the recruiting and join-up of new employees. On boarding of new employees does not end when the employee accepts your offer and arrives on site. The investment made by both parties during recruitment is significant but just the "initial" investment. From day one it is imperative to offer a structured, clear and interactive process in the presentation of New Employee training. It's developed using multimedia software with the intent of facilitating group interaction. It is more specifically aimed at providing condensed insight in some areas, and more detailed information in others, into what your company is about, it's unique product line, and growth plans etc.

A Few Focus Areas:

- Company History & State of The Business

- Product Line Overview

- Plans & Benefits Overview

- Pay & Progression System Overview

> Advancement Process/Criteria
> Feedback System

- Mentor Designation & Join-up

  > Philosophy
  > Group & One-One Join-ups

Employers implementing our vision will target and actively recruit potential employees who have demonstrated (while interning or during the hiring process) an ability to effectively multi-task. The workforce will be significantly leaner and therefore each team member <u>must</u> be multi-skilled. This will be true at every level of the workforce. The successful manufacturer will provide at least one mentor to each new employee. The new employee's progress/success will be a factor in the mentor's job performance evaluation resulting in an increased commitment to successful on boarding.

The mentors will ensure that there are aggressive training development plans in place and that timely and accurate interventions happen when needed. The mentors simply support the efforts of the managers/leaders that have direct responsibility for the new employees.

Consumers are more demanding than ever. They expect and demand world-class quality at reasonable prices. More to the point, they demand value. Companies that deliver the total value, ultimately succeed. This alone is reason enough to empower all employees to contribute to their fullest ability. Therefore, new employees should be given capable, assertive, caring mentors to provide advice and direction. They should act as liaisons to ensure that all needed training occurs. New employees should be joined-up with their mentors early during orientation. They should ve regularly scheduled meetings.

The mentors should also report to the immediate manager of the new employee regarding progress, issues, and needs. Design a plan for monitoring progress and set up frequency.

Chapter 8
High Performance
Work Systems
The "Operating System"
For Results Oriented, Collective Groups of Singularly
Focused Individuals

Key Concepts:

- Team Work
- Converting to High Performance Work Systems

For many of the people entering today's workplace, being a part of a team is a totally new experience. It is very, very important that the concept of a collective group of people working toward the attainment of common goals be systematically and methodically explained and institutionalized.

The importance of Diversity moves center stage. The unique skills and experiences of each team member compliments and enhances the company's skill base. This becomes a second family environment, and as a result, people will have disagreements, personal issues and personal successes. All employees must be equipped with the skills to handle all of the above.

High Performance Work Systems (HPWS) have at the core of their foundation the knowledge and practice that "self-sufficient teams" are absolutely vital to business longevity. Important not just for sustaining business at the current level, but also technically and socially empowered people are industry's most essential source of capital. They enable true growth/expansion capabilities.

It is absolutely critical **before** making the transition to this concept that the **highes**t levels of management be fully committed to "Work Force Empowerment" starting at the **lowest** possible levels.

Each team member is trained and evaluated. They demonstrate the ability to assume responsibilities that have been traditionally handled by managers. This is a joint venture between management and hourly employees and as a result all parties are responsible for each other's success. The entire work force is focused on achieving shared goals.

It's called "**Team Work**." As this work culture evolution occurs, managers will "cut the umbilical cord" and begin to focus more on up-stream projects and activities that facilitate business expansion. Ultimately, employees develop careers and a strong sense of loyalty to the company.

Initial Focus Areas When Considering HPWS Conversion:

- Pilot Cell Selection
- Team Structure
- Team Training

In the American Work Place of the future, traditional lines between management and non-management will be blurred by design.

At any given time any and all team members will be able to "seamlessly" move in and out of each other's roles.

Business leaders will reward not only the "technical masters" but also require them to exhibit true and complete leadership abilities such as:

- Team Building
- Conflict Avoidance & Resolution
- Team & Individual Improvement
- Personal & Inter-personal Problem Solving

These "High Performance Work Teams" will have the capability to not only operate production equipment, they will also effectively maintain, reconfigure, and troubleshoot (mechanical, electrical, process etc.) all equipment without external support. They exist without the full time presence of the traditional manager/supervisor. These are truly self-sufficient work teams. High Performance Work Systems don't just happen, this is a continuous process.

Planning The Conversion:

Carefully thought-out strategies in the area of planning key activities must be in place **prior** to concept implementation.

There is no work system that can survive and flourish without total buy-in or support from management (top to bottom). **This concept is no different!** In an effort to facilitate a smooth transition to **HPWS**, we are recommending several pre-conversion steps.

These key steps include:

1. Select one specific department in which to conduct the Pilot Cell

2. Create a "Steering Team" to guide the evolution of the concept

3. Develop Team Structure (Core and Support)

4. Develop Schedule (with time lines) for the entire Pilot Cell

5. Conduct HPWS Training with Steering Team

6. Conduct HPWS Training with ALL Pilot Cell Team Members (share logistics)

7. Deploy Teams, Measure Results, Attain/Retain Excellence

Step #1 – Select one specific department in which to conduct the Pilot Cell.

Selecting the Pilot Cell:

One indisputable way to gauge the success of converting your business to High Performance Work System is to initially select the right starting place. Ideally, a department with:

    A. High profit potential
    B. Low productivity (non-machinery related)
    C. Positive minded employees

It is also important to consider the size (number of people & amount of machinery) when making this decision. Select a department or component of a department that is manageable based on the number of resources assigned to support the effort.

By initially choosing a department that has unrealized profit potential, the organization is better positioned to influence acceptance of concept through sharing of results. History shows that everyone wants to be associated with success and the prominent posting of results will showcase improvement.

Step #2 – Create a "Steering Team" to guide the evolution of the concept.

Steering Team:

Convene a team of managers/leaders from each "support group" i.e.. Shipping, Safety, Accounting, Manufacturing etc., to serve as the directors of this effort and share general plans for converting to HPWS. This is information sharing **ONLY** at this point. Steering Team will receive formal HPWS Training later but prior to "Core Teams."

This team will have ultimate responsibility for guiding the evolution of the concept. Responsibilities include but are not limited to:

• Ensuring compliance to company policy

• Identifying and removing barriers/bottlenecks to the success of this endeavor.

• Reviewing results and intervening where and w! ɔn needed in a timely manner

• Act as mentors to members of Pilot Cell Team

The selection of truly committed members to this team is key to the successful evolution of HPWS.

Ensure that potential Steering Team Members are passionate, flexible, have a mentoring spirit and embrace positive change. Ideally, they should be volunteers and well respected specifically in their respective departments, and in the total organization as a whole. **DO NOT** omit representation from any essential support department.

Step #3 – Develop Team Structure (Core and Support)

Developing Team Structure:

Once the pilot cell "starting place" has been determined, we will create the team structure. Another way of looking at this is to decide on roles and responsibilities. We will have only "necessary" roles with clearly defined responsibilities from top to bottom. Again, only the required roles necessary to effectively operate and sustain a robust team will be initiated.

All logistics such as Team Meeting Schedules, Agenda, Results Tracking Methods, and Team Improvement Plans will be outlined. Team structure will include the make-up of not only the "Core Team" but also, the Supporting Teams i.e., Maintenance, Quality, Safety, Material Handling etc.

It is imperative that roles be clearly reviewed, understood and refined **before** "Core Teams" begin HPWS Training. Initially, management may determine who fills key roles within the teams. However, in the future teams should be allowed to determine who will be in specific roles and on what frequency they rotate. Again, **ONLY** fill the required roles at this time and as skills increase reevaluate team needs.

Step #4 – Develop Schedule (with time lines) for the entire Pilot Cell.

Develop Pilot Cell Schedule:

Set a specific span/period of time in which the pilot cell will be conducted.

Along the way, be sure to set "milestones" and share results with the entire operation. Usually, three months is a good ballpark timeframe. The schedule should cover Initial Kickoff, all HPWS Training Dates, Steering Team Meetings, Information Sharing Meetings, Team Meetings and projected date of conclusion.

If the opportunity is there, begin to disseminate information to the organization about plans to convert to HPWS weeks before the transition begins. This will facilitate dialog and interest within members of the organization, culminating in an anxiousness to discover more about the concept.

Step #5 – Conduct TBWS Training with Steering Team

Conduct HPWS Training with Steering Team:
With **ALL** members present, the Steering Team will receive training on all aspects of HPWS Methodology. This is usually a one-day training activity, and is combination lecture and group participation.

Steering Team receives the same "classroom training" as the Pilot Cell/Core Teams. **In addition to the HPWS Training**, be sure to identify any issues that have the potential for negatively impacting the conversion process. This degree of cohesiveness within this team will make or break the concept. Make an accurate determination as to whether Team Building is required.

During this time the team should have decided on a meeting schedule and <u>documented</u> any known issues.

Step #6 – Conduct HPWS Training with ALL Pilot Cell Team Members (share logistics)

Conduct HPWS Training Pilot Cell Team:
With **ALL** members present, train participants on Methodology. This is a one-day training activity, and is combination lecture and group participation. The team gets its first opportunity to see and participate in organized team activities.

Participants will be expected to participate in all aspects of training such as Role Playing, Technical & Interpersonal Problem Solving, Giving and Receiving Feedback, Goal Setting etc. Team Members will come away from this training with a vivid understanding of what it means to be a real team and share a common focus.

Step #7 – Deploy Teams, Measure Results, Attain/Retain Excellence

Teams officially begin working under HPWS Concept. All identified roles are functional and results are tracked on a shift-by-shift basis. Steering Team tracks results and provides leadership, mentoring and support. It is important that teams receive "proactive" support from all Steering Team Members and their respective departments.

Support means but is not limited to:

- Technical Resources available in non-emergency and emergency Situations

- Management working across disciplines to facilitate training

- Obstacles are identified and removed

- Information sharing is embraced and automatic

Now that you have on-boarded employees into your High Performance Work System, you must train these individuals so you can maximize their contributions to your manufacturing operation. The next chapter steps you through the key components of Technology Transfer and Training Support Systems.

Chapter 9
Technology Transfer and Training

Key Concepts:

- Performance Support Systems
- Training Development System

A Performance Support System is the accepted and institutionalized process for developing and delivering all "technical training" to the organization. It is applicable to the "core business" training requirements of any manufacturing organization. This training program is reliable, sustainable, easily upgraded, focused on desired "outcomes" and results in accelerated, ongoing skills development. This process focuses on a **specific, desired outcome**. This training concept is designed to provide the end user with all key information necessary to operate, troubleshoot and maintain equipment within the limits of equipment design specifications.

Initial Focus Areas:

- Developing Training Developers
- Standardized Training Deliverables
- Validation & Continuous Improvement

In the future, the American Manufacturer will assume a different role as it relates to the traditional customer/supplier dynamic and we see this unfolding today. Traditionally, the American Manufacturing way of doing business has been to develop a product and "push" it out to the customer. This concept has often resulted in products that did not meet the customer's requirements and therefore, they quickly disappeared from the market.

The new dynamic is one in which the customer/retailer "pulls" manufacturing along by demanding products be made to their (customer) specifications and at a rate and cost that they are willing to pay. Businesses that are willing and able to make this transition will succeed and others will not. As a result, successful manufacturers will be innovative, flexible and lean. It becomes imperative that all members of the workforce be provided with the most current technical training specific to their areas of responsibilities and that this is an institutionalized component of the organizational structure.

In addition to providing human resource training and operating principles, manufacturing organizations will know what 'technical" deliverables are essential to success and have a system for maintaining, updating, demonstrating mastery and deploying to the workforce. These training deliverables will be primarily web based and in a user friendly and self taught format.

TRAINING DEVELOPMENT PROGRAM

The establishment of a formal Training Development Team/Department is an absolute must if the full benefits that are associated with **a solid Technology Transfer and Training Program** are to be realized. Training Teams vary in size and "technical" depth, but at a minimum, we recommend the development and implementation of the following roles:

*** ROLES ***

TRAINING DEVELOPMENT DIRECTOR

This is the single point contact for the entire training development effort. This role interacts with resources associated with the successful "technical" delivery of the project. Specifically, providing guidance and support to Training Developer(s), Technical Feature Developer(s) as well as cultivating relationships with the technical, operational, engineering, and vendor communities.

TRAINING DEVELOPER

This role has responsibility for the development of complete and technically robust course curriculum. This includes instructor's guides, manuals, multimedia presentations etc. It requires working with *Technical Initiative Developer(s)* to acquire technical documents such as Present Best Techniques's (PBT's), Preventative maintenance (PM's), Job Safety Analysis, Job Aid's etc.. These documents will be an integral part of the training package.

TECHNICAL FEATURE DEVELOPER

The person in this role will shoulder the responsibility and accountability for precise development and dissemination of all feature related procedures vital to equipment removal/installation, set-up, repair and troubleshooting.

In order to facilitate consistency, brevity and accuracy, these procedures will be developed via "standardized" templates and made available to whoever needs it.

ALWAYS Train ONLY What Needs To Be Trained:

In the past many organizations have trained employees in areas where they did not really need training. Often the opportunity to use this training did not occur until long after receiving it. Here is an appropriate use of the expression "use it or loose it." Future manufacturing constraints will demand that we train specifically what is required to successfully execute the tasks before us.

Training System Components

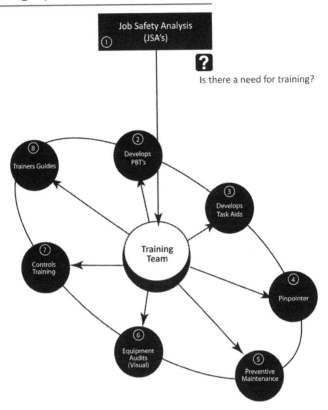

TRAINING SYSTEM COMPONENTS

This program will facilitate the creation and development of robust Technology Transfer & Training Packages that are thorough, "technically" reliable and reflect current learning's.

The curriculums should include the following tools:

- Instructor's/Trainer's Guides

- Job Safety Analysis (JSA)

- Present Best Techniques (PBT)
   A. Equipment Installation/Removal
   B. Equipment Set-up
   C. Equipment Rebuild

- Operational Task/Job Aid's

- Pinpointer

- Preventive Maintenance

- Equipment Audits

- Operator Interface

TRAINER'S GUIDES

This is a trainers "cue card" format that sequentially guides and prompts the trainer as to What points to make and When to make them. They enable focus and ensure that all "key information" is covered. Another advantage of

Trainer's Guides is the reduction in variation of content transfer. Through the use of Trainer's Guides, information transfer remains relatively identical. These tools are absolutely imperative.

JOB SAFETY ANALYSIS (JSA)

JSA's are formalized tools (documents) used to determine whether a need exist for a NEW safe practice. They identify hazards (real and potential) that operators, mechanics and electrical personnel should be made aware of in order to prevent injuries. This document MUST be completed as early as possible prior to the development of the course curriculum.

TROUBLESHOOTING

Troubleshooting Guides are developed to assist the end user in identifying and correcting outages. They begin with a single, concise statement that defines or describes the problem. They are intended to offer logical, most probable causes for outages.

PRESENT BEST TECHNIQUE (PBT)

This is a formalized tool (document) designed to aid in executing tasks that are done on an infrequent basis and subsequently, too detailed for memory. They include Safety Precautions, through, detailed execution steps, graphics, and digital photos. They should be placed in an electronic and or manual repository to enable utilization by all who need them. It is vitally important that PBT are reviewed & updated as appropriate. PBT's should be written for those tasks that carry a high consequence of error.

OPERATIONAL TASK/JOB-AID'S

There is a close similarity between Job-Aid's and PBT's. However, they are employed in very different ways. We utilize Job-Aid's for those tasks that are done on a routine/regular basis but are to complex for memory. We utilize PBT's for tasks that are infrequently performed, but if performed incorrectly, have the potential for disastrous results.

EXAMPLE: (PBT)

A rotating sheering device needs to be rebuilt (device is rebuilt in house). It weighs 2,000 lbs. and cost $58,000.00. It must be removed from production line via fork truck. To safely and reliably remove and replace this equipment takes a minimum of five (5) hours at a lost production cost of $25,000.00. Therefore, it is imperative that sheering device be rebuilt correctly. (High consequence for error)!

EXAMPLE: **(Job-Aid)**

A copier experiences paper jams several times a day. The paper path is full of flips and turns. An appropriate job aid would be to put numbers or letters at key spots throughout the paper path. These locations are displayed on the copier operator panel.

PINPOINTER

We employ the use of Single Messages as "News Bulletins" to quickly convey new learnings that would be of immediate importance. This information will ultimately be included in the appropriate document (PBT, Job-Aid etc.). This tool is only intended to be used when there is "breaking news" regarding materials, safety, equipment health etc.

PREVENTIVE MAINTENANCE

Technology Transfer & Training should be inclusive of detailed equipment PM procedures such as.

- Lubrication (type, frequency, amount etc.)
- Inspection (visual & audible)
- Process Cleaning

The information detailed in these procedures should reflect input from the most "technically" reliable sources known. Whenever possible, there should be collaboration between experienced operators, mechanics and engineers.

EQUIPMENT AUDITS

These are "Visual" equipment inspections, usually performed by the operators or mechanics. Equipment life cycle data influences what and when activities occur. With information obtained from these robust audits, technical resources are better equipped to make appropriate equipment health decisions.

OPERATOR INTERFACE

Operator Interface deals with providing training on how to operate the "controls" for the equipment. Also included in this training is. . . .

EXAMPLE:

WHAT happens when electrical/electronic devices (buttons, touch pads, switches etc.) are engaged or turned vs. the theory behind it.

Technical Mastery is facilitated by having operators, mechanics, electricians etc. understand what happens when these actions occur. Whenever the opportunity lends itself to the use of "simulators" of any kind, seize the opportunity! Often computer software programs exist that may be loaded on PC's to allow for better simulation activities (especially valuable when actual equipment is not accessible).

During Classroom Training the target audience/participants should be provided as many "visual Aids" as possible. This may be accomplished via "hands-on" exposure to actual machinery, or components.

Part Four
Putting it all Together

Chapter 10
Taking Your Company There

Key Concepts:

- Big Bang
- How can your company make the journey
- How you will know its too late for your company

Manufacturing is evolving from a single-focused mechanistic model into a system model characterized by self-improving networks and feedback loops. [3]

Manufacturing in the US has experienced on average a 1.2% productivity improvement each year from 1949 - 2001. [4]

Manufacturing accounts for three-fourths of U.S. exports and the majority of private-sector R&D. It also accounts for 13 percent of our (US) GDP and 11 percent of employment. [5]

You've finally reached the last chapter and now what? You're wondering why have we led you to this last chapter? Is this the chapter where we reveal the Future of American Manufacturing? This book has demonstrated lessons from the past such as America as a center for innovation and the impact of the capital markets and access to capital. We also stepped you through the change into systems thinking and building a system so consumers can create what they want. Now let's play it forward. We know the past, we are living the present so here is what we see in the future.

> **The future is more of the Consumer being the craftsman and designing products for themselves. Manufacturers will create the system for consumers to create what they want.**

American Manufacturing has no future. I'll repeat American Manufacturing has no future. Not there won't be any manufacturing done in America, however, the future of Manufacturing in the America will be the same as the future of Manufacturing in all other countries. This future involves all the concepts we discussed in the book:

1) INNOVATION
2) ACCESS TO CAPITAL
3) TOP DOWN THINKING
4) ACCELERATED NEW PRODUCT LAUNCHES
5) SYSTEM LEVEL PEOPLE SYSTEMS

> **American Manufacturing has no future. Not there won't be any manufacturing done in America, however, the future of Manufacturing in the America will be the same as the future of Manufacturing in all other countries.**

The reason we say that American Manufacturing has no future is because America does not have exclusive rights to these five items.

Innovation: No one owns Innovation. Innovation comes from all over the world, however, America leads in innovation partially because of our culture and its society of free thinkers. Will this change? It does not seem likely that the U.S. will lose its innovation lead even as democracy is spreading around the globe.

Access to Capital: The world capital markets are well developed. As a leader in innovation, this provides the capital to get new innovation out to market. Therefore, this is a self sustaining loop. Whatever company has the lead in innovation, will shortly gain the lead in access to capital. Innovation without access to capital, is like blinking in the dark. No one sees it and no one knows you even did it.

Top Down Thinking: Any organization around the world can implement Top Down Thinking by designing a **Marketing Oriented Manufacturing/Consumer Driven Product System**. A Marketing Oriented Manufacturing/Consumer Driven Product System is a manufacturing infrastructure driven by the innovators that are making a match between the needs of the market/consumers and what is possible to manufacture. Marketing Oriented Manufacturing Systems will be vital to the success for manufacturers in the future because the future of American manufacturers lies in four core areas and the manufacturing companies that support these four core areas.

> **A Marketing Oriented Manufacturing/Consumer Driven Product System is a manufacturing infrastructure driven by the innovators that are making a match between the needs of the market/consumers and what is possible to manufacture.**

Core Area 1 – Manufacturers in the Balancing Equation/Delivery Optimization

Manufacturing facilities located optimally between resources/raw materials and customers/distribution networks balanced against the total delivery cost. Some high volume products with a significant amount of labor costs will be manufactured oversees and shipped to the American consumers. Key factors in location of manufacturing facilities will be the cost of raw material, cost of energy, workforce and land. This balancing equation/product delivery optimization will be in all industries. It is already happening in some industries. It is an evolution instead of a revolution and the evolution has already begun.

Core Area 2 – Manufacturers in the Top 5% of Capabilities

These manufacturers have the equipment, processes, expertise and/or systems that other manufactures do not have. These top 5% of capabilities can do work that other manufacturers in America can't do and in some cases, some manufacturers around the world can't do. In some cases, these top 5% of capabilities manufacturers have patents on some technologies or processes.

Core Area 3 – Specialty or Niche Manufacturers

These manufacturers typically own specialty or niche Brands. They typically do not have any special manufacturing capabilities, however, these manufacturers are successful in marketing their products. These specialty or niche products are generally characterized by lower unit volumes, but typically higher margins. All around the world, if you have a core competency of marketing and sales, you can stay in business regardless of the business environment.

Core Area 4 – Accelerated Product Launch Organizations

These manufacturers have built systems optimized to quickly get new product ideas to the market. Some may argue that manufacturers in this core area are a subset of the manufacturers with in the top 5% of capabilities. In some cases, this is true, however, the manufacturers in the top 5% of capabilities have not optimized their whole operation to get new product ideas to the market. The reason why this core area will remain in America is because new product development leverages past innovation. As long as America is leading in innovation, America will also lead in number and capabilities of accelerated product launch organizations. Currently, there is a lot of innovation sitting on the shelves of many large manufacturers because these innovations do not fit their system. At large manufacturers, their systems call for delivery of products that have a high volume, high net outside sales and high margins. This is why these accelerated product launch organizations can provide a profitable platform for these innovations with market opportunities too small for large manufacturers, but may have a market opportunity of over $5 MM/year. This leads into the next discussion of the future of American Manufacturing, licensing innovation.

The reason why this core area {Accelerated Product Launch Organizations} will remain in America is because new product development leverages past innovation.

Innovators

	Manufacturing	Engineering	Marketing & Sales
Balancing Equation/ Delivery Optimization	✓	✓	✓
Top 5% of Capabilities	✓	✓	✗
Specialty or Niche	✗	✗	✓
Accelerated Product Launch Organizations	✓	✓	✓

(Manufacturing Core Groups vs Innovator Groups)

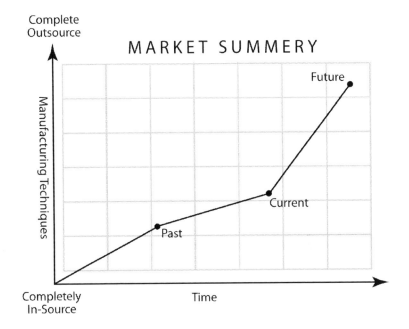

New Product Development

The Past

- Large companies had capability to develop new products and bring them from idea to final large volume production.

- Small companies struggled to bring ideas forward because of issues with cost of capital and lack of experienced resources.

- Inventors had no way of easily pulling together the expertise to launch product ideas.

- Companies requested product ideas be more complete before they were willing to invest in them.

The Present

- Companies are willing to contract out more of the early development work. Internal expertise of larger companies is dwindling.

- Large companies are leveraging their core competencies of marketing and distribution and are willing to purchase product and brand ideas.

- Inventors with great concepts have a need to move the concept forward with financial backing but lack development and manufacturing capability to produce the product.

- Small companies are investing some money in ideas and get them started.

The Future

Large companies, small companies, and inventors will increasingly demand a flexible, efficient, and responsive means to supply consumers with products that meet their unmet needs.

Challenges in the marketplace	Opportunity for Accelerated Product Launch Companies
Because of cost of capital companies find manufacturing small-medium production runs cost prohibitive.	They can manufacture at a lower cost point, thus generating profitable business for us and a profitable product for our customers to sell.
Companies have difficulty moving from product design to consumer testing.	They have a flexible, small system to move rapidly through all phases of the product cycle.
Because of functional lines within companies, the product design needs to be changed throughout the process.	They design products to progress through the product progression to full scale manufacturing.

Innovators are at the heart of each core group of manufacturers.

- Manufacturers in the balancing equation/delivery optimization group are generally created by large innovative companies developing these large market opportunities.

- Manufacturers in the top 5% of capabilities are generally built by manufacturing or engineering innovators.

- Manufacturers in specialty or niche markets are generally created by marketing/sales innovators.

- Accelerated Product Launch Organizations are typically created by the innovator's innovator.

These organizations are meeting the needs of the market by creating a system to speed the launch of innovation into the market.

American manufacturers, as well as manufacturers all around the world, have started realizing that it can be better financially to license innovation and other intellectual property, than to manufacture. As long as you own the intellectual property (Brand name, process, methodology, etc.), why do you need to tie up cash in capital equipment, workforce, infrastructure, etc.? It is estimated that worldwide licensing revenues exceeded 150 billion in 2002. [1]

Accelerated Product Launch Organizations are typically created by the innovator's innovator. These organizations are meeting the needs of the innovator market by creating a system to speed the launch of innovation into the market.

Licensing revenues will continue to grow at an accelerated rate and will be a growing part of the future of American manufacturing. That's why innovation webs are developing where companies tie into self organizing network of value creators so innovation becomes collaborative, distributive and open. Without these networks, many new products will not be delivered to the market place because no one company has the intellectual property, systems and workforce to go it alone. Whether this innovation takes place oversees, collaboratively, the owner(s) of the intellectual property is the winner. That's why a big part of the future of American manufacturing is licensing and not producing the end product. Licensing will still produce cash (access to capital) that can be invested in launching additional innovation…creating a self sustaining loop.

Now comes the uncomfortable part of the chapter.

Is your company within any one of these four core groups?

Are you are a manufacturer that fits within the balancing equation?

- Are you a contract manufacturer that is optimally positioned between raw materials and the current distribution network/consumers for your product?

- If you currently are a balancing equation manufacturer, what happens if/when the distribution network/consumer trends change?

- Can another manufacturer in your vicinity take your contract because they can offer more value?

Are you a manufacturer in the top 5% of capabilities?

- Do you own machines that no one else in the US has or machines that very few other manufacturers own?

- Do you have patents on some manufacturing processes or products?

- Do you have economies of scope in your industry where no one else can produce a product near your cost structure?

Are you a manufacturer of a niche or specialty product?

- Do you own a Brand?

- Do you have a license or contract to exclusively manufacturer a product?

- Do you provide a customized product?

Are you a manufacturer known for Accelerated Product Launch?

- Are you known for new product launch in your industry?

- Is your organization optimized for getting product ideas to the market?

- Does your organization have the equipment, processes and expertise to take a new product to the market faster than your competitors?

If you're not in one of these four core groups, are you a manufacturer that supports other manufacturers in one of more of these core areas? Are you a supplier to the automotive industry, supplier to the consumer product companies, etc.?

The only problem with not being in one of these cores is that you are further down the supply chain….in other words a secondary manufacturer. Yes, a secondary manufacturer and you have much less control over your future. As a supplier, you can more readily be replaced and driven out of business. The only way of securing your future is by being in one of these four core groups.

> **The only way of securing your future is by being in one of these four core groups.**

Now some of you are feeling <u>very uncertain</u> about your future. If you are not in these core areas, you need to take actions to either get into one of these core groups or focus on how you will solidify your supplier relationships and stay in business. However, some of you suppliers are in the top 5% for the service you provide.

For those of you who want to take action, here is how you get into one of these core groups.

Core Area 1 – Manufacturers in the Balancing Equation/Location Optimization

As a contract manufacturer you may be able to manufacturer a product within your area of expertise to get into this group. However, being in this core group is related to your facilities location in relation to the raw materials and distribution network/consumers of the product.

Core Area 2 – Manufacturers in the Top 5% of Capabilities

If you're not already in the top 5% of capabilities, this is the hardest core group to get into. Manufacturers in this group have generally invested capital over years and decades into their capabilities. Without significant strategic investment, it may be impossible to get into this group.

Core Area 3 – Specialty or Niche Manufacturers

Entering this group has the lowest barriers to entry. Building a brand or purchasing the rights to manufacturer a product are the best strategies to entering this group. However, in order to be successful in the area you have to have strong marketing and sales competences. If you do not have these types of competencies internally, partner with other companies to be successful in this group.

Core Area 4 – Accelerated Product Launch Organizations

This core group is only for organizations with product development expertise in a particular product area or industry. Expertise can be obtained by bringing on the right key individuals, however, this type of organization must have a visionary at the helm that truly understands product development for that product area or industry.

Notes

[1] "Realizing the Power of Innovation Webs", *Optimize Magazine,* December 2005.

[2] Dan Dimancescu & Kemp Dwenger, *World-Class New Product Development:Benchmarking Best Practices of Agile Manufacturers*, American Management Association, 1996.

[3] "Manufacturing Trends", *Northern Great Plains, Inc.,* 1997.

[4] Multifactor Productivity Trends in Manufacturing, *US Dept of Labor,* 2004.

[5] "Manufacturing and the Future of the American Economy", *National Association of Manufacturers*, 2005.

3295159

Made in the USA